Alexander

Pichushkin

The Shocking True Story of The Chessboard Killer

Roger Harrington

Table of Contents

Introduction

Born into a poor family in a cramped apartment in forgotten Moscow suburb Alexander Pichushkin would achieve something that none of his contemporaries in the Konkovo District would ever manage. His actions between 1992 and 2006 ensured that his name would go down in history. To some he is the Bitsevsky Park Maniac. To others he is the Chessboard Killer. To the people he grew up with he is Alexander 'Sasha' Pichushkin an ordinary boy who would become one of Russia's most feared serial killers.

After his father left Alexander Pichushkin grew up in a single parent family. Initially a shy child a playground accident turned him into an angry young man, unable to control his temper. This event also helped to turn Pichushkin into an outsider. As the child became increasingly unhappy his mother, Natasha, ran out of options. It was then that her father, Alexander Pichushkin's grandfather, stepped in. For the next few years Pichushkin lived with his grandfather and learnt how to be a man. He also learnt how to play chess and drink vodka.

After the death of his beloved grandfather and loyal pet dog Pichushkin found himself to be increasingly isolated. By now he was once again living in a cramped apartment with his mother and half-sister. During this period Pichushkin took to drinking heavily and looking at pornography. It is reported that he also found enjoyment in scaring the young children who played in the nearby Bitsevsky Park.

A few months after his 18th birthday Alexander Pichushkin committed his first murder, brutally

killing a school friend, Mikhail Odichuk.
Despite investigating the police did not have
enough evidence to charge Pichushkin so he
was allowed to go free.

Soon after Pichushkin left school he got a job
working in a local market. After finishing work,
he would return home to drink, consume
increasingly violent pornography and follow
the trial of Andrei Chikatilo, a recently caught
serial killer. Pichushkin soon became fascinated
by Chikatilo and started to fantasize about
committing similar crimes.

On the 17th of May 2001 Alexander Pichushkin
entered Bitsevsky Park with a chilling purpose
in mind. Here he selected a lonely and
vulnerable drunk by the name of Yevgeny
Pronin. Pichushkin lured Pronin into a quiet
corner of the wooded park where they shared a

drink. Pichushkin then beat Pronin senseless before dumping his lifeless body down a nearby well. This pattern was one that Pichushkin would deviate little from over the next few years. It is thought that at least sixty people met their ends in this way. Despite the effectiveness of this method two people are known to have escaped from Pichushkin's clutches however due to the inept local police force he was allowed to remain at large, free to kill again.

Eventually the act of murder would not be enough to satisfy Pichushkin. He soon realized that he needed to be noticed for his crimes. In November 2005 Pichushkin killed former policeman Nikolai Zakharchenko. However unlike in all his previous attacks he did not dump Zakharchenko's body into the well, instead he left it out in the open expanse of the park, waiting to be discovered.

When it was the reaction was swift. The police launched a manhunt as the locals and press speculated over the serial killer in their midst. The killer was quickly dubbed the Bitsevsky Park Maniac. Pichushkin was thrilled. Despite the intense police presence, he continued to kill, leaving the bodies of his victims strewn around Bitsevsky Park.

Eventually, the murder of Marina Moskalyeva in June 2006 led police to Pichushkin. After his arrest, he proved surprisingly eager to talk. The reason for this is that Pichushkin wanted the acclaim; he wanted his total of kills to be higher than that of his inspiration Andrei Chikatilo.

During the police search of the family flat they found Pichushkin's chessboard. On this board he would careful black out the white squares, one for each life he had taken. This led to Pichushkin being dubbed the Chessboard Killer.

Eventually Pichushkin was sentenced to life in a high security, remote Russian prison. To his eternal frustration Alexander Pichushkin was only convicted of the murders of forty-eight people, five less than Chikatilo. That there is no clear reason why Alexander Pichushkin committed all these murders only makes his crimes more disturbing. In interviews Pichushkin had claimed to neither regret nor repent his actions, and says that even if he did it wouldn't change anything.

Alexander Pichushkin's Early Life

The Konkovo district of Moscow. Around half
an hour from the bustling center of the city.
Like many of Moscow's suburbs, this was
where the ordinary people lived. Those who
were neither rich nor powerful. The workforce
that powered the Soviet machine. Often these
districts were forgotten, overlooked by the
establishment but for those that lived there,
these tightly knit communities were home.

The year was 1963 when, along with her family,
11-year-old Natasha Pichushkina moved into a
two-bedroom apartment on the fifth floor of 2
Khersonskaya Street. The building was almost
completely identical to all the other blocks in
the district and beyond, the dull uniformity a

preferred feature of the Soviet state. These five storey buildings were known by Muscovites as Khrushchovki, named after then premier Nikita Khrushchev. They were the Soviet Union's first large scale public housing projects. The basic buildings were dark, damp, charmless, and overflowing with tenants. Despite this they had an appeal for many, they were the first single family homes that they had ever lived in, they were an improvement.

From Natasha's new home it was a six-minute walk to the north end of Bitsevsky Park. For many the nearby Bitsevsky Park was their escape. The park measures roughly 3000 acres, extending from Balaklavsky Prospekt, a boulevard on the north end, to the MKAD, the multi-lane highway that encircles Moscow, four miles south. It is an enormous expanse, for comparison New York's Central Park covers only 843 acres. The park itself is a long expanse of largely beautiful forest filled with streams and clearings. In the winter time the park is a popular site with cross country skiers.

The charm and enchantment found in the park was in stark contrast to the projects that surrounded it. The natural greenery is surrounded by tens of thousands of people living in sprawling, rusting apartment blocks speckled with satellite dishes. For many lives here was a meagre and basic one but it was the only life they had ever known. Many people call this grim, concrete part of Moscow the zhopa mira, or "arsehole of the world."

1963 was a year of change not just for Natasha and her family. The Cuban Missile Crisis came in the middle of a period of de-Stalinisation instigated by the then President Khrushchev.

For those who had grown up in the strict confines of Stalin's Russia this was a confusing time with no clear future. Many saw the liberalization of their country, as something to be feared not welcomed.

The people who lived in Khersonskaya Street were similar to those in all the other apartments in the Konkovo district and indeed all the other similar Moscow suburbs. People would be born here, they would live out their lives working and raising a family here and here they would die. Often their lives would be lived without having ever left their small area. The residents may not have agreed but to all intents and purposes, it was a de facto prison.

For Natasha her life was to take an all too similar course. She grew up on the Konkovo streets and eventually fell in love on them.

When her son Alexander was born Natasha's parents moved out, ceding their daughter the flat. While her parents remained close by Natasha's home became her son's home. This was all too common a story for the people of Konkovo.

Eventually as Natasha's family grew Alexander would sleep on the couch in the first bedroom, which doubled as the living room. Natasha slept alone on a queen size bed ten feet from her son. In the master bedroom slept Pichushkin's younger half-sister, Katya. Later Katya's husband, also named Alexander, and their son, Sergei, affectionately called Seriozha would share the room. It may seem a cramped existence but for many it was the only one they knew. This familiarity provided comfort in a quickly changing world.

Later this familiar, safe neighborhood would become Alexander Pichushkin's hunting ground. Ten of his victims would come from the area around Khersonskaya Street. People he had known since childhood. The innocence of Bitsevsky Park shattered.

Alexander Pichushkin was born on the 9th of April 1974. His mother would affectionately call him Sasha. Before Alexander reached his first birthday his father had left, abandoning his son, his name now lost to history.

A few years later Natasha met another man. However, he also did not stick around for long, just enough time for Natasha to fall pregnant. Soon Katya, Alexander Pichushkin's half-sister was born. When she was old enough Katya got the flat's sole bedroom, Natasha converted part of the living room into a sleeping space for herself and her son. This was a common practice in Khrushchovki Street and the surrounding areas.

As far as we know Natasha was a good and caring mother. She spent most of her time tirelessly working to provide for her children. This meant that Alexander and Katya missed out on quality time with their mother, however, Natasha's parents, the children's grandparents, remained close at hand and helped out as much as they could. We can also be fairly confident in saying that neither child suffered from any abuse.

Neighbours would later remember the young Alexander Pichushkin as a shy but good-natured child. He seemed no different to the other children in the area. The young boy liked to collect commemorative pins; this was a common hobby for children growing up in the Soviet Union. There were pins commemorating the 1980 Olympics in Moscow, Tolstoy pins, Lenin pins, a pin from Minsk 92, around ninety in total. When asked Natasha would describe her son as ordinary, brave and honest. Natasha later came to the conclusion that she had not raised her son very well at all, but at the time she thought she was doing the right thing.

One-day young Alexander Pichushkin's life changed forever. He was in the park playing on a swing when somehow he fell backwards off the swing. As Pichushkin sat confused on the ground the swing swung back and hit him directly in the forehead. Hard. Without money for a proper medical consultation Alexander Pichushkin was dusted down and when he could walk and see straight again was pronounced a survivor. Externally this may have been the case but soon people began to notice changes in the boy.

The previously shy child became quick to anger. Often scaring his schoolmates and friends in the park with a newly violent nature.

Years later medical experts would cite this incident with the swing as a key moment. It has been theorized that this incident damaged the frontal cortex in the still developing brain of Pichushkin.

This part of the brain contains neurons that interact with dopamine. Essentially it is the pleasure-giving part of brain, it also controls how a person deals with reward, happiness and motivation. As it is also a vulnerable area studies have been done showing that trauma here can often lead to poor impulse control and the shortening of tempers. While Pichushkin himself has never been studied, studies done on others and the observed change in him after the accident allow us to conclude that this was a key moment in his life and would have a lasting effect.

Following his accident Alexander Pichushkin began to get bullied, both verbally and physically, at school. His classmates ridiculed him for being slow, or as they often bluntly put it "retarded". Provoked Pichushkin would lash at those around him, not just his bullies. It was during this period that Pichushkin began to form his "me against the world" mindset. From now on in the tightly packed community Alexander Pichushkin would forever see himself as an outsider.

His doting mother Natasha became concerned that Pichushkin was struggling at school.

Eventually, after trying to help him herself, she opted to remove him from school and instead enrolled him at a school for children with learning difficulties. This only added to Alexander Pichushkin's sense of otherness. Despite the best intentions his new school was of little help to Pichushkin. This was largely because they were unable to diagnose just what disability the boy had.

During this period Pichushkin became increasingly withdrawn. Reluctant to attend the new school he struggled to concentrate when he did. Consequently, his education stalled. Pichushkin's grandfather noticed this. He suggested to his daughter that the young Alexander move in with him. Upon doing so the boy gained something that he had been missing for a large part of his life, a male role model.

His grandfather encouraged Alexander Pichushkin to look for fulfillment outside of the strict educational confines he so disliked. A believer in self-sufficiency Pichushkin's grandfather taught his grandson how to be a man.

Each day after school the two would head to Bitsevsky Park. In one particular corner of the park men would gather. Here they would drink vodka, talk and play chess. This quickly became a bonding activity for Pichushkin and his grandfather. It also gave the young Pichushkin a new way to see the world. It seemed that what his grandfather had hoped was correct; the exposure to other ways of thinking seemed to give Alexander Pichushkin a new interest and more self-confidence. The boy began to find himself.

For some the idea of men gathering to play chess in a park may seem strange. But it is important to appreciate that during the years of the Soviet Union the will of the individual was often suppressed, the emphasis instead was placed on the state. People were encouraged work and engage in activities that benefited the whole not the individual; the emphasis was placed firmly on the collective. This extended to many leisure activities. One of the few exceptions was chess. It was a game of skill and gave the individual a chance to shine.

Chess was perfect for Alexander Pichushkin and his almost constant state of discontent. On the surface it is a simple game but once you look deeper one appreciates how complex it is, Pichushkin saw similarities with himself in this regard. By the time he was a teenager Pichushkin was easily outwitting the older men. His confidence grew and grew as he felt domination and power. For the first time Pichushkin felt the respect of others. He had found a place to thrive.

It is fairly safe to say that this was the best time of Alexander Pichushkin's life. He found a settled routine that suited him. He would ignore his schooling, preferring instead to rush home to share a vodka with his beloved grandfather before the pair headed to Bitsevsky Park to while away the hours playing chess. For Pichushkin life was good.

However, there was one aspect of life that his grandfather did not prepare Pichushkin for. His death. The event rocked the teenager's world. With the passing of his grandfather Alexander Pichushkin lost the only positive male influence in his life and by now it was too late to find another. Pichushkin realized that from now on he would have to find his own way in life. A task for which he was completely unprepared.

After moving back into his mother's cramped apartment Pichushkin increasingly began to hide his emotions. He had few things that gave him genuine comfort- just chess and a pet dog that his grandfather had given him. The dog was Pichushkin's only true emotional bond. However, despite this, despite the close confines nobody noticed how troubled the teenager was. If they did they chose not to do anything about it. Or perhaps they couldn't.

To many Alexander, Pichushkin appeared a normal Russian teenage boy but inside he was deep in turmoil. Alexander Pichushkin's world was darkening by the day.

By now Alexander Pichushkin was supposedly attending a vocational school. In truth he spent most of his time in the park with his dog playing chess. He had also begun to drink heavily. For many Russian men drinking vodka together is a way of bonding. Pichushkin would often drink alone. Soon his neighbours noticed that he was spending his days drinking. It was not something he wished to hide.

It is likely that during this time Alexander Pichushkin also started to consume pornography. There is a school of thought that argues that if young developing minds are exposed to pornography it can rewire the brain. A young brain is still developing making it more susceptible to any outside influence. For Pichushkin who probably already had a damaged brain pornography possibly triggered in him a sense of enjoyment. Soon the pornography became more violent, more graphic.

For Alexander Pichushkin alcohol and pornography replaced any real emotional desire and empathy he may have felt. His mind became increasingly warped. After he was eventually arrested the police search of Natasha's apartment turned up explicitly violent videos. But for now Pichushkin was still sinking into depravity. Soon another event would rock his world.

The death of his beloved dog saw Alexander Pichushkin lose the only deep emotional bond he had left in this world. This loss would haunt Pichushkin for years; in the police interviews after his arrest, he would blame himself for the death of his beloved pet. Nobody knows if this means Pichushkin killed the creature himself, serial killers often start on animals before working up to humans, or whether it was killed by someone else as an act of revenge for Pichushkin's increasingly out of control behavior.

Either way, Alexander Pichushkin was now increasingly isolated. His mother Natasha and half-sister Katya either couldn't or wouldn't talk to him. Bitsevsky Park became his haven, more home than his family's cramped apartment. With no positive emotional bonds, Pichushkin was adrift. Unchecked he let rage fill his life.

It is reported that in his later teenager years Pichushkin started taking a video camera to Bitsevsky Park. He would take delight in scaring the younger children and filming their horrified reactions. One, extreme, story tell how on one occasion Pichushkin dangled a child out of the window by his ankles. As the child squirmed and screamed Pichushkin took great delight in explaining to the terrified youngster how his life was entirely in Alexander Pichushkin's hands.

The rush of power he had first felt when winning chess games Alexander Pichushkin now felt again. Greater than before. For a while this was enough to satisfy him. But not for long. Soon Alexander Pichushkin would look for a greater thrill. He started to formulate a plan to murder someone.

The outsider began to observe those around him, identifying other lonely outsiders. Weak and vulnerable people who would not be missed. Soon he was ready.

Alexander Pichushkin's First Murder

1992. The year Alexander Pichushkin turned 18. For a young Russian, it was a turbulent time to come of age. The securities of the Soviet Union had collapsed. The Berlin Wall had come down. Boris Yeltsin's government was in the process of opening Russia up to the wider world. For those who were used to the securities of the old world, this new dawn was as much something to be scared of as it was to be excited by.

That year, on the 27th of July Alexander Pichushkin asked a school friend, Mikhail Odichuk, to accompany him on a "killing expedition". The pair attended the same vocational school. Neither were marked out for greatness, instead they were expected to learn some form of trade. After leaving school they would embark on a life of service, probably earning very little and with little chance of improving their fortunes. Odichuk and Pichushkin were classmates; to call them friends may be an exaggeration. As we were to later see Alexander Pichushkin had few if any friends or close relationships. He would only grow close to someone if he felt that they could be of use to him, often by becoming yet another one of his victims.

One-day Alexander Pichushkin had boldly told Odichuk that he intended to kill somebody. When he realized that Odichuk was not going to inform someone in authority or was to stop him he had invited Odichuk to accompany him. It is probable that Pichushkin was intrigued by Odichuk's reaction; maybe he hoped that he had found a kindred spirit. Someone who felt the same urges and desires, a willing accomplice to help him on his quest. For his part Mikhail Odichuk had agreed to the invitation probably half in jest, not really believing that Alexander Pichushkin intended to murder somebody.

As the two young men walked along the oblivious Moscow streets Pichushkin started to point out possible victims; these were people he identified as being weak or vulnerable, people that probably wouldn't be missed by anybody anytime soon. Slowly Odichuk realized that his classmate wasn't joking. Pichushkin genuinely intended to commit murder that afternoon. Scared Mikhail Odichuk tried to make an excuse, he had to go home.

Pichushkin knew that Odichuk was lying; perhaps he could see the fear in his companion's eyes. He wasn't interested in Odichuk's increasingly desperate excuses. Pichushkin firmly insisted that his friend stay.

This did little to calm Odichuk who was increasingly horrified with the unfolding situation. It was then that Alexander Pichushkin turned. He knew now that Mikhail Odichuk was not a kindred spirit who, like himself, desired the thrill of a kill. Instead of attacking one of the many potential victims he had earlier identified Pichushkin turned his rage onto his friend. Young Mikhail Odichuk was murdered in cold blood.

Alexander Pichushkin fled the scene in fear. Soon the teenager's lifeless, battered body was found. An investigation was launched. The police asked questions. All roads led to Alexander Pichushkin.

They found that Pichushkin had been with Mikhail Odichuk on the day of his death. The talk amongst the youngsters was that Pichushkin had been friends with Odichuk. There was also talk of Alexander Pichushkin's quick temper and violent tendencies. Despite this there was no real proof.

The police interviewed Alexander Pichushkin but he denied everything. They had no actual proof just a series of suggestions and rumors. It wasn't enough. For a police force constrained by boundless reams of red tape any actual investigative work was far more trouble than it was worth. Unless they found firm proof quickly the police officers found it easier not to bother, to hope that it wouldn't happen again or that an informal chat was enough for lessons to be learnt. As Mikhail Odichuk was buried the investigation was dropped, Alexander Pichushkin remained a free man.

It seems that for a while this was enough. By his own admission, Alexander Pichushkin wasn't to kill again for nine years.

We do not know whether this was because his bloodlust was properly satisfied or whether the terror of almost getting caught was enough to stop him from killing again, at least temporarily. It is not uncommon amongst serial killers for the stress of the kill, especially the first kill, to be enough to stop them for a while. One murder does not necessarily open the floodgates to further kills. It is possible that the experience, the thrill of the kill followed by the encounter with the police and the realization of what he had done spooked Alexander Pichushkin. For a while the young man may have tried to suppress his urge to kill. Whatever the reason Pichushkin now entered his dormant period, he would not kill again for nine years.

Instead Alexander Pichushkin left education and got a job as a shelf stacker in a nearby market. It seems that this was enough for him. He had no further ambition than this or at least not visibly. In his head Alexander Pichushkin was becoming increasingly consumed with thoughts of murder. When not going over the death of Odichuk he was planning his next kill. It was also during this time that Alexander Pichushkin became obsessed with the Rostov Ripper.

Known as the Rostov Ripper, Andrei Romanovich Chikatilo was born on the 16th of October 1936 in Yabluchne. While then part of the Soviet Union today Yabluchne is in Ukraine.

Primarily active in the Rostov district, hence his nickname, between the years of 1978 and 1990 Andrei Chikatilo committed the sexual assault, murder and mutilation of at least 53 women and children. Today he is considered to be one of the most prolific serial killers to have ever operated either in or outside the Soviet Union. The full horror of his many crimes only became known after his arrest.

He was eventually put on trial for the murder of 53 people. Andrei Chikatilo's trial, which began in April 1992, gripped the Soviet Union. Many were appalled and sickened by the graphic nature of his crimes. In October 1992 he was found guilty of these crimes. As the death penalty was still in force in Russia at the time Andrei Chikatilo was subsequently executed in February 1994.

During this fallow period Alexander Pichushkin's life fell into a set pattern. After finishing work Pichushkin would head home where he would spend the night drinking and consuming copious amounts of pornography and the latest details from the trial of Chikatilo. It is believed that by reading and watching the reports of the trial, which graphically detailed Chikatilo's crimes, Pichushkin got a vicarious thrill. It was maybe an effective substitute for the thrill he had experienced when he killed Odichuk. If this were the case, then the vicarious thrill would not be enough for long.

Many believe that through studying the details of Andrei Chikatilo's crimes as well as learning how he managed to evade justice for so long Alexander Pichushkin was serving a form of twisted apprenticeship. Pichushkin would later say that he killed to live. Or to put it another way Alexander Pichushkin found that the only time he felt truly alive was when he was taking the life of another. This is something he learnt was possible from studying Chikatilo. Pichushkin also learnt that it was possible for a serial killer, if they were careful enough, to remain free and active for many years and possibly decades. Eventually Alexander Pichushkin resolved to become more prolific than Andrei Chikatilo.

This sort of competition is not unusual amongst serial killers. Between May 2005 and August 2006 in Phoenix, Arizona in the United States two serial killers were found to be operating at the same time. The killers became known as the Serial Shooters. Their activities followed a noticeable pattern. The police discerned that after one had killed the other would strike in response; it was as if they were spurring each other on. Incidentally a third serial killer, Mark Goudeau often referred to as the Baseline Killer, was also active in Phoenix during this period but his activity does not seem to have been influenced by the Serial Shooters.

For Pichushkin Andrei Chikatilo became his inspiration. He became determined to get more kills that the Rostov Ripper. Alexander Pichushkin believed that this would be easy, in his mind he was a genius (his success at chess told him this) it should, therefore, be easy for him to kill more than a peasant like Chikatilo.

So, like the chess grandmaster he believed himself to be, Alexander Pichushkin waited. He studied his potential victims, working out who were unlikely to be missed should they one day vanish. With his victims in mind Pichushkin devised a plan, simple but clever enough to leave no trace or sign that pointed back to him. He found a place to commit his heinous crimes and an ideal location to dispose of the bodies. Then and only then the time was right. Alexander Pichushkin emerged from the shadows ready to claim his place in history as the Chessboard Killer.

Bitsevsky Park

On the 17th of May 2001 Alexander Pichushkin returned to Bitsevsky Park and the familiar corner where the men whiled away their days playing chess. Yevgeny Pronin was, like Pichushkin, a park drunk living on the outskirts of society. After playing a few games, and probably winning as he usually did, Pichushkin started to talk to Pronin. This conversation confirmed to Pichushkin what he had already observed- that not many people would notice were Pronin to disappear. Being careful to make sure that they were not being observed by anybody who would remember Pichushkin invited the man to walk through the park with him. Alexander Pichushkin told Pronin that it was the anniversary of his beloved dog's death and he wished to visit the grave.

Whether it really was the anniversary or not we do not know but this excuse was one that Alexander Pichushkin would use time and again to lure his unsuspecting victims to an isolated corner of Bitsevsky Park.

When they reached the lonely spot Pichushkin produced a bottle of vodka and offered Pronin another drink. The man did not decline. They drank a toast to Pichushkin's lost pet. Now drunk and isolated Pronin was helpless when he noticed a change in the demeanour of his companion. Alexander Pichushkin became hard, cold. He turned on Pronin.

While we don't know what Pichushkin's chosen weapon was on this occasion we know that later on he would often use metal rods or even the vodka bottles themselves to smash the skulls of his victims. After battering Pronin to helpless unconsciousness if not actual death Alexander Pichushkin stopped. He coldly hauled Pronin's lifeless body to the nearby well and dumped the body down it. Pronin's body plummeted thirty feet into the dirty waters below. If the man weren't dead from his injuries the almost inescapable water would soon end his life.

The well Pichushkin dumped his victims down fed into the large and winding Moscow sewer system. If the bodies ever washed up in a place where someone would notice them, and that in itself was a big and unlikely if, they would be unlikely to trace them back to Bitsevsky Park.

This pattern, of carefully identifying and then luring an isolated and lonely member of society to this quiet corner of the park before attacking them and dumping their body into the well, would be one that Alexander Pichushkin would follow almost rigidly for much of the next five years. But that was all in the future. Following the death of Yevgeny Pronin Alexander Pichushkin found that killing came easy. Over the next eight weeks he would lure nine more unsuspecting victims to their watery deaths. It is now known that many of those dumped down the well by Pichushkin were not dead merely unconscious. Unable to get out, a struggle not helped by their injuries, they subsequently drowned in the darkness.

With the body disposed of Alexander Pichushkin would embark on the next part of his kill ritual. Being careful to make sure that he was not observed leaving the area Pichushkin would hurry home to his family's cramped flat where he would retreat to the privacy of his bedroom. Here he would carefully take out his prized possession- a chessboard. Alexander Pichushkin would carefully black out one of the white squares every time he killed somebody.

At the start Pichushkin's victims were similar. They were usually pensioners or tramps. The forgotten or unregarded of society. People who, when they disappeared nobody would notice that they were gone. If a family member did care enough after waiting the requisite three days they would make their solemn way to the police station where they would file a missing person's report. Here, the police, known more for their drinking and bribe taking than detective work, would read the report and forget about it. If you were lucky they filed, it away for future reference. No one made any connections or noticed that the number of missing people being reported was increasing. Nobody cared.

Amongst the residents there were rumors. Some of the vanished were rumored to have moved away, others were speculated to have had run ins with the Chechens or the Mafia. A more fantastical rumor speculated that an escaped mental patient was loose in the area. By the middle of 2003 some of the families were beginning to wonder whether it was someone they knew. Some had noticed that the missing all came from the same area. They also knew that in a society like theirs few people mattered, them and their relatives were definitely not in this category.

Ultimately nobody knew, and few cared enough to learn.

Alexander Pichushkin's initial spree culminated on the 21st of July 2001 with the disappearance

Victor Volkov. His disappearance went largely unnoticed.

Those who did realize either didn't know what to do or didn't care enough to do it. Volkov's whereabouts was discussed amongst the gossiping neighbors for a day or two if that. They speculated that he had moved away, to a new job or to be with family. Maybe he had been hospitalized or arrested. There were theories but nobody had the desire to find out the truth.

Unbeknown to them all he had become Pichushkin's eleventh victim. As autumn turned to winter Alexander Pichushkin continued to kill sporadically, the frenzy of his initial spree had faded somewhat. Five people fell prey to his murderous ways during this period, possibly more. On the 23rd of February

2002 Maria Viricheva came to Alexander Pichushkin's attention.

Viricheva was an incomer to Moscow. Originally from a rural part of Russia where work was hard to come by Viricheva had followed a familiar route. Realizing that the only way to support herself was to move to Moscow, and bitterly aware that she could not afford the necessary expensive work papers and permits, Viricheva had instead entered the city as an illegal immigrant. Here, in the shadows amongst other illegal immigrants and criminals, she found life to be poorly paid and hard. Despite this, she told herself it was better than the life she had left behind in the countryside.

The nature of her lifestyle meant that Viricheva was isolated from society, unable to trust those around her in case they discovered her secret and betrayed her to the authorities. When she met Alexander Pichushkin she had been living this lonely lifestyle for a while. Viricheva was also pregnant. This did not put Pichushkin off.

As always he befriended her, it is possible that she was glad of his company. She may have been told the story of his beloved dog and, feeling sympathy for the awkward young man, agreed to accompany him to the grave to mark the anniversary of the creatures passing. Whatever the reason she willingly accompanied Alexander Pichushkin to the isolated corner of Bitsevsky Park. Here Pichushkin offered Viricheva vodka, all too aware of her condition she refused. Undeterred Pichushkin took a drink himself before striking the woman over the head with a blunt object. His attack drove her, terrified, stumbling backwards towards the well.

Pichushkin took his opportunity and shoved Maria Viricheva down into the dark, watery depths. Satisfied that his job was done Alexander Pichushkin turned and made his way home. Hours later Maria Viricheva tired and in pain, slowly climbed back out of the well. The exhausted lady then slowly made her way to a hospital desperate for help and safety.

When the police arrived at the hospital to question Viricheva she was able to provide them with not only a detailed description of the attack but also of her attacker. If they had acted on this information, then the police would have been able to stop Alexander Pichushkin's murderous spree. Instead they asked to see Maria Viricheva's papers.

Worried about what was going to happen to her Maria Viricheva tearfully admitted that she did not have any. The woman, who had already gone through one incredibly stressful ordeal that day, now began to fear that she would be deported from the city, or worse imprisoned. The police officers, wary of the paper work all this would bring, gave Viricheva a choice. They informed her that they would ignore her illicit presence in the city if she dropped her claim that she had been assaulted.

Reluctantly Viricheva agreed, she had no choice as she had to continue earning money to support her family. So the woman stayed in Moscow, but from now on she avoided the Bitsevsky Park area as best she could. For their part the police had missed another opportunity to catch Pichushkin and stop his murderous spree. We do not know if Alexander Pichushkin was aware of Viricheva's escape. If he was he certainly didn't pursue her. Instead Pichushkin found more victims, over the next two weeks three more people would meet their end in Bitsevsky Park.

Maria Viricheva was not the only person to have a lucky escape from Alexander Pichushkin.

To get to and from his place of work Alexander Pichushkin traveled on the metro, getting on and off at the Kakhovka Prospekt stop. It was often a busy place with people, usually youngsters and teenagers, hanging around. It was an ideal place for Pichushkin to watch and observe, identifying his next victim. A common sight at the locations hanging around the flower stalls, food stands and kiosks was a group of punk skateboarders. The group would vary in size day by day, depending on who wanted to hang out. They often shared around paper cups filled with vodka, hoping the police would not notice.

One day Pichushkin noticed one of the youngsters, Mikhail Lobov. He was a 13-year-old skater boy and well outside Pichushkin's usual target range. He was not elderly, isolated from society or a resident of Khersonskaya Street or its surrounding area. It is possible that Pichushkin targeted Lobov as revenge against the type of teenager he never was, the type of teenager who would gleefully taunt the outsider.

Whatever the motive Pichushkin tempted Lobov to Bitsevsky Park with the promise of vodka and cigarettes. While the victim was unusual the routine was frighteningly similar.

After twenty or so minutes of walking they stopped. Pichushkin offered the young man a cigarette and vodka. He made small talk, probably trying to impress Lobov and then when the boy was least expecting it Pichushkin hit him over the head with a surprise blow and pushed him down the well.

Like in the early attack on Maria Viricheva Pichushkin now left the scene, not bothering to hang around. He was confident that he had killed again. If his assault hadn't been enough the fall into the watery depths would surely be enough. Alexander Pichushkin, for the second time, was wrong. If he had hung around Pichushkin would have seen that Mikhail Lobov's jacket had caught on a piece of metal inside the well saving him from a plunge into the icy waters.

Eventually, after much struggling, Lobov was able to climb out. Scared and unsteady the boy found a policeman and informed him of the assault. Like Maria Viricheva, Mikhail Lobov was able to describe the assault and his assailant in detail. However, the policeman wasn't interested. He had no time for a trouble making kid pestering him late at night. Even if the policeman had believed Mikhail Lobov it is unlikely that a jury would have.

Over the next few days Mikhail Lobov lived in fear, terrified that his assailant would learn that he had survived and hunt him down. Soon fear turned to determination. Lobov would not be afraid. He wanted justice. Accompanied by his friends Mikhail Lobov returned to the metro station. There the group waited until they saw Alexander Pichushkin alighting from the train before starting on his way home. Lobov excitedly informed a nearby police officer.

Again Mikhail Lobov found himself ignored but he was not to be easily deterred. Lobov began screaming and clawing at Pichushkin's hair. When this didn't work Lobov proceeded to grab one of the officers standing outside the station and started pointing and shouting, telling the officer that they had to do something. They did; the policeman pushed Lobov away and told him to go home before he arrested him. Pichushkin continued on his way home no doubt relieved. Again the police had missed a chance to catch the serial killer.

It would be another four years and many more bodies before Alexander Pichushkin was finally stopped.

There is a story told about one day in either 2001 or 2002 at a time when Pichushkin had killed somewhere between twenty and thirty people. It is said that a drunken Alexander Pichushkin stumbled into his local police station. There he loudly proclaimed to have killed many people and would continue to do so for as long as he is able to because "that is what I must do". Instead of taking his drunken claims seriously the on duty police officers laughed Pichushkin out of the station, thinking him to be nothing more than a deluded drunk.

While this is yet another frustratingly missed opportunity it was not unusual. In the small and impoverished communities, some would say forgotten communities; on the outskirts of Moscow the police regularly turned a blind eye to crimes. While the Soviet Union was long gone the red tape that had held it together remained. They found that the bureaucratic system was too complex and time consuming to negotiate; instead an almost lawless society, which policed itself, emerged. Due to the attitude of the police it became clear to the killer that the only thing that could stop Alexander Pichushkin was Alexander Pichushkin himself.

If this story of the drunken Pichushkin is true it strikes the casual observer as strange. Why would you admit to such crimes if you had no real need to? He was not a suspect, there was no evidence and Pichushkin was not being questioned. The police did not even know that a serial killer was in operation.

The only logical conclusion that can be drawn is that deep down Pichushkin had a desire to be recognised as a more prolific killer than Andrei Chikatilo. While he was certainly more prolific nobody knew who he was. This drove the confession. Soon this deeply hidden desire would come to the surface.

Increased Savagery

Surprisingly Alexander Pichushkin's favourite book was How To Win Friends and Influence People. In this regard he is not alone amongst serial killers. Charles Manson also used the book to his own ends, helping him to manipulate his family and those around him. For Alexander Pichushkin How To Win Friends and Influence People gave him an insight into the western world, a world where your intelligence and determination could allow you to move up in the world.

This was far removed from the crumbling Soviet society Pichushkin had grown up in, where who you knew was more important. People were encouraged to work for the betterment of the collective as opposed to the individual. There was no real opportunity for personal advancement. Despite the title of the book Alexander Pichushkin didn't really have friends. Nor did he want them. He had victims. Pichushkin would often only get close to people in the moments before he killed them; this gave an added edge to the murder, a bigger thrill.

By now Pichushkin's sister Katya was married, to a man also named Alexander. The couple shared Katya's bedroom at 2 Khersonskaya Street with their young son. There were now five people living on top of each other in Natasha's cramped flat. To an outsider an environment such as this would seem an impossible one in which to keep a secret.

If Alexander Pichushkin was displaying signs of living a double life, as some serial killers do, it was so crowded in the small flat that it would be almost impossible not to notice. However, this was not the case. Alexander Pichushkin was not living a double life. He had one life where he worked by day and killed by night, and nobody cared enough to notice the signs or to stop him. Whatever he was physically doing in his head Alexander Pichushkin was always planning his next kill.

The spring of 2003 found Alexander Pichushkin on the lookout for his thirty second victim. He soon found him. The man was a local and a drunk, like many of his previous victims and like Pichushkin himself. Pichushkin spent time watching the man sit alone in the street, smoking and drinking. He kept up this watch until he was sure that the man would not be missed. Then Pichushkin approached. A brief conversation confirmed what Pichushkin already knew, that the man was alone.

The victim was also angry. So much so that for the first time Alexander Pichushkin worried that his chosen target may not comply or worse, try to fight back. Pichushkin need not have worried; the offer of free vodka was too tempting to the drunk. Soon they were in the woods heading towards Pichushkin's favourite spot.

When they finally stopped walking the men shared the vodka bottle. Pichushkin asked his companion if he had a wish. The man replied that he wanted to stop drinking. Alexander Pichushkin calmly told him that today would be the day he stopped. He then struck the man with the bottle. The brutal assault continued, caving the defenseless man's skull in. Finally, Pichushkin shoved the vodka bottle into an open wound in the skull. He then dumped the body down the well and left.

Over the years Alexander Pichushkin's attacks had become increasingly violent. But by now violence itself was not enough. Pichushkin was getting sloppier. It has been theorized that this is possibly because subconsciously what Pichushkin really wanted now was to be known for his crimes. For his name to eclipse that of his hero Chikatilo.

One cold night in November 2005 the police were called to Bitsevsky Park. A body had been discovered. Nikolai Zakharchenko was 63. He was also a former policeman. It has been suggested by some who have taken an interest in the case that Pichushkin picked this particular victim, and left his body out in the open air waiting to be discovered, as a challenge. Despite the two surviving attack victims, the numerous unexplained disappearances and the years of whispered rumors nobody in the police force had ever really bothered to look at the mysterious happenings in Bitsevsky Park. With the discovery of Nikolai Zakharchenko body that all changed. He was Pichushkin's forty first victim.

If the discovery of Zakharchenko sparked the police into action it also prompted an awakening amongst the people who lived in the surrounding Khrushchovki. On the icy streets and in the dark, damp buildings people gathered and began to discuss the murderer. They recalled the names of people who had vanished across the space of so many years, adding to the seemingly ever growing list of potential victims. As realisation dawned terror began to ripple through the apartment blocks and metro stations that surround Bitsevsky Park.

The park itself, once a place to escape and relax, now felt grim, haunted. Children were forbidden to venture into the woods. Those who did venture into the park claimed to hear shouts and cries echoing through the trees. That was when the moniker Bitsevsky Park Maniac entered the local lexicon. It soon spread to the Internet and the wider world.

A manhunt for the killer was launched. Alexander Pichushkin had his wish, the spotlight was now firmly on him and his deeds. One night Alexander Pichushkin, his mother Natasha and half-sister Katya were watching the news when a report about the Bitsevsky Park Maniac came on. Pichushkin noticed how involved Katya was in the report. She would obsess over every clue, speculating endlessly on who the killer may be. Katya had no idea how close to the truth she was.

As Pichushkin watched his sister he felt butterflies. He knew that a word from him would solve her mystery. Satisfy her desire. He had to fight hard to keep his ghastly secret to himself. This gave Pichushkin a huge thrill; the excitement the speculation generated gave him satisfaction. His risk taking personality found satisfaction in this moment.

Soon, spurred on to gain greater notoriety, to fuel the speculation further Pichushkin found that recklessness became its own reward. He continued to kill. Reveling in the spotlight his crimes drew. In no time at all Pichushkin was leaving bodies in the snow covered open of Bitsevsky Park. Sometimes the corpses would be found propped up behind trees.

The worst, it was reported, came early one morning. A doctor was walking his dog when, by the banks of a river, he came across a pack of wild dogs fighting over some bones. As he got closer the man realized that the bones the dogs carried in their mouths were human remains.

Like the press and the public, the police had also realized that there was a serial killer on the loose. They were also aware of how long they had ignored the reported disappearances and rumors for. Questions were asked, how many people had died needlessly? This drove the detectives on, determined to stop the deaths. Despite this newfound determination it was obvious to everyone that Pichushkin's victims had been failed by the system. Pichushkin had been allowed to get away with his crimes because of the time in which he lived. His desire to kill exceeded the system's ability to notice him let alone stop him.

If Pichushkin had stuck to the same routine of dumping bodies out if sight in the well he may never have been caught. He could even be still active today. Unnoticed apart from the gossiping residents of the Khrushchovki speculating that they had a killer in their midst. It was only when the disappearances turned into murders too obvious to ignore, did anyone pay Alexander Pichushkin any attention. By then, for forty one people, it was far too late.

Despite the increased police presence dead bodies continued to turn up. Enquiries were made but nobody had seen the victims entering the park or the woods with anyone in the hours before their death. Alexander Pichushkin may have got bolder but he was still being careful, old habits die hard. The size of the park also helped Pichushkin; it was so large that the police found it nearly impossible to patrol the entire park constantly. Frustratingly for them, however hard they tried, there would always be blind spots.

Deep down Alexander Pichushkin must have realized that the end was near. He must have sensed that the civil war inside him was reaching its apex and that soon he would do something stupid and they would find him. You can't carry on for as long as this without making a mistake. But, many have speculated, maybe Pichushkin wanted to get caught. Despite being more prolific he was in the shadows of Chikatilo and other serial killers. To fully get the notoriety that he felt he deserved he had to be known. That meant he had to be caught.

As the story grew the powerful Interior Ministry took charge of the case. Andrei

Suprunenko was placed at the head of the investigation. He enjoyed catching killers, especially serial killers. He was good at it.

After reviewing the evidence Suprunenko and his team came to a frustrating conclusion, ultimately without a new slip up or further insight they were stuck. Not to be deterred Suprunenko gave the police at his disposal strict orders. They were to work hard. Determined to force the mistake.

While the bodies continued to turn up with a grim regularity the police, some in uniform, some in plain clothes, patrolled the park as best they could. Others worked to narrow the search, interviewing everybody. They gathered descriptions and compiled sketches, drew up a profile of their killer. They may not have known his name but they were quickly getting a picture of the killer. Time was running out for Alexander Pichushkin.

However, at the end of the day despite the efforts of Suprunenko, the police and the victim's family and friends they still couldn't catch the man dubbed the Bitsevsky Park Maniac. Instead it was Alexander Pichushkin who delivered himself into the hands of the police.

Pichushkin's Arrest and Conviction

On the 14th of June 2006 Marina Moskalyeva followed the usual pattern her life had fallen into. She got up and sent her son to school before heading to the grocery store where she worked. Before Moskalyeva started work at the store another woman, Larissa Kulagyina, had worked there. One night on her way home she had disappeared never to be seen again. Moskalyeva may not have known about this but, like the rest of Moscow, she had heard of the Bitsevsky Park maniac. It is therefore all the stranger that she agreed to go for a walk in the park after work that night with her colleague, Alexander Pichushkin.

Despite being keen to get home and start preparing tea for her family Moskalyeva agreed to accompany Pichushkin on a walk. Maybe she felt sorry for him, having heard his story about the cherished dog buried in the park. Before they left Moskalyeva had returned to her flat and left her son a note telling him where she was going and with who. She also put Pichushkin's phone number on the note. Later her son returned to an empty flat and read the note.

After a while, when his mother had still not returned the boy turned on the television. It was a news bulletin; they were reporting that a woman's body had been found in Bitsevsky Park. The boy rang Pichushkin, concerned and wondering where his mother was. Pichushkin told the boy that he had not seen Marina Moskalyeva in two months and, claiming that he was too busy to talk to a child, hung up. Worried the boy rang his father. After listening to his son the father rang the police and informed them of the note.

Andrei Suprunenko realized immediately what this meant. The note itself was interesting but not damming. The CCTV footage of Marina Moskalyeva and Alexander Pichushkin getting off the metro and heading in the direction of Bitsevsky Park added weight to their case. Suprunenko was thrilled but also surprised at just how easy Pichushkin had made it for them. For his part Pichushkin knew that this would lead the authorities to him but he just couldn't stop himself. He had tried, fought with himself on every step of that walk through the park. However, in the end it made no difference, Marina Moskalyeva had to die.

Two nights later as the clock approached midnight the adult residents Natasha Pichushkin's flat in 2 Khersonskaya Street were preparing to go to bed. They were disturbed by a knocking on the flat door. This in itself was odd- you had to ring a buzzer to gain admission to the building. Assuming it was a neighbor in desperate need Natasha cautiously opened the door. The sight that greeted her is one she will never forget.

A column of men dressed in riot police uniforms pushed past her into the tiny flat. Within minutes Alexander Pichushkin had been arrested. They told the prisoner's worried mother that they just wanted to question him in connection with a series of burglaries. Later Natasha would come to see this as a kindness on the police officers part, that they didn't want her to learn the horrific truth in such a cold manner.

Alexander Pichushkin was escorted away from his home to a police cell. Meanwhile the police remained in the flat, searching for evidence. It was then that they found Pichushkin's chessboard, sixty of the sixty-four white squares had been coloured in. This piece of evidence would later give rise to Pichushkin's familiar moniker, 'The Chessboard Killer'.

Meanwhile his elderly mother was in shock. Natasha found it hard to settle or to focus on what was happening in her home. She was upset by the presence of the police in what she believed to be a law abiding home. It was while watching this that the truth dawned on Natasha. She realized that Alexander

Pichushkin, her little Sasha, may never be a free man again.

Before the sun had risen word had started to spread around the tight knit housing blocks. Natasha Fyedosova, whose father Boris was Pichushkin's thirty sixth victim, recalled later there "was total shock when we heard it was Sasha Pichushkin". She recalled the serial killer as "always very calm, always by himself." Fyedosova, who grew up with Pichushkin's half-sister, Katya, and had known Alexander Pichushkin for almost all of her life, determinedly attended all forty-six days of Pichushkin's trial. "I thought it was strange that he only wanted to kill people he knew," she would later confess in an interview. "If he had killed people he didn't know, in another neighbourhood, it wouldn't have been as bad, but he killed people he knew."

Andrei Suprunenko would spend the next few months questioning Alexander Pichushkin. As a result, the interrogator probably knows him better than anyone else, including Pichushkin's family. It took some time to establish a relationship but soon Suprunenko got Pichushkin to talk.

For hours the two men would sit in one of the holding cells, Suprunenko on one side, Pichushkin on the other, under fluorescent lights, smoking. Alexander Pichushkin had the habit of wandering when he spoke, meandering in and out of his exploits. Suprunenko says he always stared straight at Pichushkin. "It made him feel important," he says. "I told him I admired him, and he liked that, and then he opened up. It was very important for Pichushkin that people think he was a hero, so I made him feel like a hero."

"We were in shock when we realized how many people he'd killed," Suprunenko later recalled. "In the beginning, we only had thirteen bodies. And then Pichushkin began to tell us that he'd killed more than sixty people." Pichushkin opened up about everything, the location in the park and the convenient well. As Pichushkin talked Suprunenko began to understand the fates of all those people who had disappeared. "He wanted to talk," Suprunenko says. "All maniacs want to talk."

Later Suprunenko would reveal that he believed the Chessboard Killer moniker to be misleading. He is sure that Pichushkin would have been unable to stop once he reached sixty-four- the number of white squares on the board. When asked what sort of person Alexander Pichushkin was Suprunenko answers quite simply, the famed Bitsevsky Park Maniac was completely ordinary. He didn't have strong opinions. He lacked preferences or ideas about other people, God, art, beauty. He could talk about these things, and did, but these were simply words in the service of killing; they were bits of theater; they were nothing.

Psychologists who examined him concluded that Pichushkin was narcissistic and had a personality disorder but, ultimately, was sane. "For the serial killer, the process of preparing to kill and killing is an erotic experience," says Alexander Bukhanovsky, a psychiatrist and serial-killer expert who had helped authorities identify Pichushkin's hero Chikatilo in the early 1990s. But the sex act itself is not erotic for serial killers, Bukhanovsky says. For serial killers what is erotic is killing and all its associations, the mental links and symbols of murder. For Pichushkin this meant the biting wind in the evening, the shadows and birds and birch trees, the crunch of ice and branches, the kaleidoscopic splatter of an old man's blood on fresh snow. Pichushkin himself would admit that he sometimes climaxed during the act of killing.

Suprunenko exploited Pichushkin's narcissism. For a killer so hard to catch building up the case was easy. Alexander Pichushkin gave them information because he wanted them to find the bodies. He wanted to make sure that his kill total was as high as possible. He needed to beat Andrei Chikatilo. If he hadn't needed the validation of the wider world, to feel the attention of the world on him, Alexander Pichushkin may have remained free and undetected for many more years.

There have been suggestions that Pichushkin was homosexual. This speculation has been denied by those who knew him. Natasha Fyedosova recalled that Alexander Pichushkin never had any interest in girls and never talked about sex or looked at women the way boys and men often do. Despite this lack of interest in members of the opposite sex she doesn't think that Pichushkin is gay.

This opinion is shared by his mother, Natasha. "My son was actually going to marry someone," she says. Despite her sons announcement Natasha never met Alexander's bride to be. She probably didn't exist. Andrei Suprunenko, the detective who led the Pichushkin investigation for the prosecutor general's Department of Homicide and Armed Robbery in Moscow, also rules out the possibility that Pichushkin was homosexual.

Instead he believes that he just wasn't interested in women, this is a view shared by Bukhanovsky.

Russia, more so when Alexander Pichushkin was growing up, is a largely illiberal country, especially when compared to its western European neighbors. Here much emphasis is placed on the strong man. Much of Russian society is largely homophobic. Those who are gay try to hide it; unsure of whom they can trust. They know that it is better to deny themselves than be outcast from society, however painful this choice is. In such a society people can easily believe that a gay man is not a real man. It has been suggested that the vehement denials that Alexander Pichushkin is homosexual come from an ingrained disbelief that a gay man is incapable of exerting the power or force thought necessary to kill.

Ultimately however Alexander Pichushkin's sexuality makes no difference. He is like so many of the other men from the Konkovo and all the other Moscow suburbs. Indeed, like many young men from all over Russia. He is rough, crude, a heavy drinker and chain smoker. He has no expectation that he will ever be able to better his lot, any dreams he had of doing so died a long time ago. He will probably die before he reaches the age of sixty- the average life expectancy for Russian men is somewhere in the late fifties a symptom of a people who are prone to all kinds of self-abuse and have, at best, spotty health care. He doesn't have a career nor any hope of attaining one, if he is lucky he has a job. Expectation and hope for a better life died long ago.

What marked Alexander Pichushkin out from the so many others who were just like him was how he reacted to the realization that he had been discarded by society. Instead of grudging acceptance or working hard to prove the world wrong or making sure that the next generation would not be so cruelly denied Pichushkin chose another path. He found a way to make sure that his name would forever be etched in history, never forgotten. Better to be feared than forgotten. If society didn't want him then he would exist outside it. Alexander Pichushkin chose to kill.

Pichushkin's confession was aired on Russian television. For the ordinary Muscovites who had lived in fear of the Bitsevsky Park Maniac this was a must watch event. In it, he discussed at length his need to kill. "For me, a life without murder is like a life without food for you," Pichushkin reportedly said. Showing no remorse, he later argued that he should be charged with more murders, keeping with his claim of killing sixty-one or sixty-three people (his story varied). "I thought it would be unfair to forget about the other eleven people," Pichushkin reportedly later commented during his 2007 trial.

Every day during Alexander Pichushkin's trial the court was packed. Except for his poor mother, who was still in shock unable to comprehend what Sasha had done and blaming herself, almost everyone else from his neighborhood attended. Many came on a regular basis.

The people who lived on the outskirts of society found themselves sitting in the recently renovated Supreme Court of Russia, on Povarskaya Street in the center of Moscow, at odds with their usual surroundings. If they felt out of place here it didn't show, they were too determined to hear Pichushkin's story to worry about such trivialities. They needed to learn what had happened to their family and friends, the neighbors who had just disappeared. More importantly they wanted to know why.

Each day, upon entering the court, Pichushkin was greeted with the same sight. Standing before him would be his lawyer Pavel Ivannikov, the judge and jurors, the prosecutor in his royal blue military-style uniform, the babushkas who lost sons and husbands, the younger men and girls whispering into their cell phones, too scared to look at the Bitsevsky Park Maniac, the man that until recently they called neighbour. Alexander Pichushkin, like Chikatilo, was kept throughout the hearing in a reinforced glass cage. This was primarily done for his own safety. However, it also served to further mark him out as an outcast, different and shunned by the rest of society.

On the 24th of October 2007, Alexander Pichushkin was found guilty of murdering forty-eight people. It took the jury only three hours to come to their conclusion. That he was found guilty of killing only forty-eight people is significant. The number is five short of the total Andrei Chikatilo was convicted of. As Alexander Pichushkin was led away he knew he would never reach what he considered his potential, to eclipse the man who had inspired him.

Throughout the trial, he had insisted that he'd actually taken sixty-three lives, but the authorities could only muster enough evidence to prosecute him for only forty-eight. He was sentenced to life in prison. Since Chikatilo's conviction Russia had abolished the death penalty. Alexander Pichushkin's conviction and the revelation of the horrific nature of his crimes sparked a debate amongst many over whether the death penalty should be reintroduced.

A week after his conviction, Pichushkin's attorneys filed an appeal, requesting a more lenient sentence. On Valentine's Day 2008 the court met again. Again it was packed. The press and his former neighbours filled the space. While it seemed that the rest of his neighbourhood was present Pichushkin himself was absent, appearing instead via a video link. At one point a woman cries out "Where is my body", breaking the solemn silence. She lost her husband down a snowy path in Bitsevsky Park one winter's night. Only Pichushkin knows what happened next.

Despite the appeals of his attorney, the judges are unmoved. After deliberating for less than an hour they decline the opportunity to reduce Pichushkin's sentence to twenty-five years. Instead the sentence stands. Alexander Pichushkin will never again be a free man.

Not long after this Alexander Pichushkin was sent to a high security prison in the remote Ural Mountains. Here he will spend the first fifteen years of his sentence in solitary confinement, without as much as a chessboard for company. For Natasha to see her beloved boy she will have to undertake an arduous train ride which will last at least a day. This journey will be rare.

Today Alexander Pichushkin is regarded as a monster the world over. His crimes are a source of nightmarish terror. Pichushkin's motivations have been speculated over by numerous criminologists, psychologists, and serial-killer aficionados. Despite this speculation nobody knows why Alexander Pichushkin killed as many people as he did. This only adds to the terror of his crimes. Pichushkin is, in short, the most feared man in Russia.

Closer to home the name of Alexander Pichushkin will forever be one that is feared, especially in the tight knit communities that live around Bitsevsky Park. While they know he is safely held far away from them Pichushkin still haunts their nightmares.

Concerned parents and grandparents still keep a cautious eye on their children. The drunks still huddle closer together than before, still alone but somehow not. All are aware that what happened once could, if they are not careful, happen again. If the worst were to happen it would be the people of the Khrushchovki that would have to fight. Not just for justice but to be noticed. The people were failed by the police and the system for so long and so little has changed that they know that for all their close bonds the people of the Khrushchovki are truly alone.

Printed in Great Britain
by Amazon

68659055R00057